HEARING ECHOES

Canada Council for the Arts **Conseil des Arts du Canada**

The publisher gratefully acknowledges the support of the Canada Council for the Arts and the Ontario Arts Council for its publishing program. The publisher is also grateful for the financial assistance received from the Government of Canada.

Cover artwork: Linda Frimer, "Sunlight's Forest Dance [Keystone Project 1]," 2014, acrylic on canvas, 18 x 24 inches. Artist website: lindafrimer.ca.

Cover design: Val Fullard

Library and Archives Canada Cataloguing in Publication

Norman, Renee, 1950-, author
      Hearing echoes / Renee Norman and Carl Leggo.

(Inanna poetry and fiction series)
Poems.
Issued in print and electronic formats.
ISBN 978-1-77133-337-5 (paperback).--ISBN 978-1-77133-338-2 (epub).--
ISBN 978-1-77133-339-9 (kindle).--ISBN 978-1-77133-340-5 (pdf)

      I. Leggo, Carl, 1953-, author II. Title. III. Series: Inanna poetry and fiction series

PS8627.O763H43 2016   C811'.6   C2016-904871-3
                                                        C2016-904872-1

Printed and bound in Canada

Inanna Publications and Education Inc.
210 Founders College, York University
4700 Keele Street, Toronto, Ontario M3J 1P3 Canada
Telephone: (416) 736-5356 Fax (416) 736-5765
Email: inanna.publications@inanna.ca Website: www.inanna.ca

MIX
Paper from responsible sources
FSC® C004071

HEARING ECHOES

POEMS BY

RENEE NORMAN AND CARL LEGGO

inanna poetry & fiction series

INANNA Publications and Education Inc.
Toronto, Canada

*For my loving and awe-inspiring daughters, Sara, Rebecca,
and Erin (again, always), who fill my life with joy and laughter.
And for my mother, Shirley Silver.*

*For my darling granddaughters, Madeleine, Mirabelle,
Gwenoviere, and Alexandria, who teach me how to live poetically.*

Contents

A THOUSAND PITIES

PUTTING IT INTO WORDS

THE RELATION BETWEEN

PUTTING THE CHILDREN TO BED

She lives in you and me,
and in many other women who are not here tonight,
for they are washing up the dishes and putting the children to bed.
—Virginia Woolf, *Room of One's Own*

Dreaming Grandchildren

I look at sweet faces
your granddaughters
a photo
how fortunate they are
your devotion lit
by support of women
you shine more than a camera lens
on feminisms

I remember my daughters
vibrant toddlers
joy and chaos
now still flashes of opalescent colors
some temporary darkness

I am dreaming grandchildren
into focus
hazy visions
small ghosts
in the space between
note to daughters: no pressure, understood?
I have dresses, little ponies, flaming room
in my mother's heart
ah, granddaughters!
I promise
my two miscarried babies
taught me patience

how to release plans
like so much gossamer

some day I will show photos too

Ten Reasons Why Your Grandfather Loves You

for Madeleine

1
you sit on the rail of the bridge over the slough,
I hold you firmly with one arm,
our mouths open,
we see red-winged blackbirds like miracles
silence spills in the earth's arteries
spells the heart's endless desire

2
during our walk home
I carry you on top of my head,
when I look up
you are leaning over with a grin
that reminds me of God's

3
when you lean into me
touch me with your lips
I taste your baby's breath
like hope will fill me forever

4
you suck your toes
because you can
because you want to know
the texture and taste
of everything

5

you climb and slide
swing and walk
slip and run like
you are training
for the Olympics
and I moan I'm 55,
I can't keep up,
but you don't hear me
and I'm glad

6

you wave and smile at everyone,
especially elderly Sikh men in turbans,
and your toothy grin lights up like a neon sign
so bright you see only the light
burning from a fire that cannot be quenched

7

I want to see the world
through your eyes

my eyes are dim

you hear planes and look up
see the sweep of gulls and crows

already you know frozen peas
should be eaten only
after all the sun-kissed strawberries are gone

8

we fall back on the bed
bounce down the stairs
hop from post to post
run so fast Nana can't catch us
stroll along the dike
sit in the sand
pretend to be a plane
and in everything we do
hold fast to lines of light
connecting us and everything

9

we look in the gray eyes of the goat
inside the fence at the end of No. 2 Road,
everything is a mystery
that cannot be exhausted, only enjoyed,
so we explore without ceasing
the bountiful creation that refuses
a simple embrace

10

located in the earth, we learn
to keep the heart calling earth's rhythms
with roots seeking deep and deeper,
the whole earth sung in veins of long light
that can sustain the heart's rhythms

Last Summer of Childhood

for Erin

we are watching What Not to Wear
in pyjamas and old shorts
this her last summer of childhood
before university begins

soon enough she will be writing papers,
walking on campus in the rain,
wondering where summer went
and holding her damp coat close
to keep warm

this is my last baby
the one I rocked slowly
savouring, savouring
her faded cotton sleepers
smelling of sisters,
old milk

when we shopped at the mall
our own episode of What Not to Wear
again and again she emerged:
a white eyelet skirt,
a rust tunic
my eyes on her becoming

the transformation taking place
behind a curtain of clothes

we are watching What Not to Wear
this *our* last summer of childhood

Mirabelle

you run to me
    leap into my arms
       full of joy
    for stories

    because
you do not have
words   we read
    the texts
    scribbled between
letters   words   lines
    songs of love

always   yearning
    to learn

    one day
you will call out
    Papa

    I hope
I remember these days
when you invited
    careful attention
interpretation

    writing the unknown

line   collaboratively
    finding our way

you breathe into me
    a sentence with
no punctuation
    no capitalization

we speak
       in cipher
the body's language
      a wild imagining
beyond
      deciphering

Spill of Trees

Morning. Bare limbs on trees. Grey skies with a hint of light to come. The spectre of Spring. The circle of ice on the outdoor table melted for now. A shine of windows across the creek. Two fat squirrels heavy with maple nuts waddle across the fallen leaves now more mulch then foliage. Houses, rooftops form the backdrop for skeletal branches, criss-crossing in patterns that speak of paint spillage: random, beautiful, permanent. Here and there a hair gnarl of knotted branch. A last leaf bereft of its original shape. Still the grey light entices, reminder that winter too has more than darkness.

Last night I could not sleep, thought of daughters. How content I am they swirl around me still. In and out between their work, projects, concerns, cups and wineglasses left for parental pickup, stray underwear strewn by bathrooms, clothes left hanging to dry, the basement pantry their shop-at-home-free store (the price is right). And I would not trade one unmade bed from a sleepover, nor the blueberries that find their way under the depths of the fridge, nor the opened wine, or the cranky hurricane takeover of my bathroom, for anything else. That promise of Spring is not for bargaining. The Jackson Pollack spill of trees is only one canvas I love.

Gwenoviere

your favourite response
to any question, any event
    yeh YEH Yeh yeH yEh
repeated again and again
like you are singing scales
for a new ode to joy

in your resonant laughter
like bubbles you remind us
    YEH yeh Yeh yEh yeH
of countless reasons for hope
like an angel with a message,
both urgent and singular

you are a beacon, a light
that glows with fire
    Yeh yeh yeH yEh YEH
that disperses clouds, refuses
sadness like throwing off
a musty gray flannel blanket

you are a song of jubilation
lingering on the threshold
    yeH YEH Yeh yEh yeh
of a life just begun where
you write lines in the air
spring festival fireworks

like miracles, your cousins
call you baby, you watch
YEH yEh yeH yeh Yeh
with amused smiles, patiently
biding your time, in no hurry
to jump queues, eager to learn

you will laugh love live
with alliterative affirmation
yeh YEH Yeh yeH yEh
our lives, composed in letters
and parts of speech, calling
out stories without calculation

Gardens

I am growing a garden again
my youngest daughter
helps me pick out seeds, seedlings
map what should go where
plant what doesn't need
overnight soaking
tells me to write it down

this return to the earth
follows years of nurturing children
my own, others in classrooms,
universities

the black soil pungent
smells like the beginning of being
soaks up water on a sweltering day
like the elephants at the Calgary Zoo
greedy for liquid
spray after spray on tough dry dust hide

the pumpkin plant droops like me
in the heat of searing sun
perks up as leaves
wet
turn in supplication

I plant the beans and peas
plump
after their overnighter in water

remember my daughter's advice
my mother's lush garden long ago
the handful of dirt I sprinkled
on my father's grave

daydream about plants so close
together they strangle one another
or a bountiful harvest
I pick armloads for daughters

here in black soil
this earth womb
I plunge my hands
feel dirt enter my pores
stain me
with old rhythms
new possibilities
growing another kind of garden

Faster than a Bullet

It's a Madeleine day today. Oh, yes, it's a Madeleine day today!
Living on the moon is no fun. There's nothing to do. You can only walk around.
Can you hold this? I need one hand for my iPhone and one hand for my dolls.
Papa, French fries don't come from France. They come from McDonald's.
A ghost mummy is when a ghost and a mummy go crazy at the same time.
Whatever you do, whatever you say, don't get married next to a volcano.
Women do good stuff to their children. They keep them safe and healthy.
Please, take the crust off my bread. Nana always does that sometimes.
I don't like being a ghost. I only like being a mummy or a skeleton.
When I get to be a teenager, Daddy will let me watch *True Blood*.
Would you like this jujube? It's a little sticky, I didn't lick it.
How about next Halloween I'll be Princess Leia in a bikini?
For Christmas, I'm going to get Daddy earrings, like Papa.
Only in Newfoundland can you sing Newfoundland songs.
I don't have any germs, Daddy, do you want to try some?
I like eggs you eat, not eggs that talk. They look scary.
Papa, don't call my Daddy a horse. He's a unicorn.
Maybe I won't go looking for the Holy Grail.
I can almost run faster than a bullet.
Do you love me more than Sears?
When you die, God is your boss.
Does the Queen of England fart?
I wish all movies had a squid.
Did I shrink?
It's a Madeleine day today. Oh, yes, it's a Madeleine day today!

Beached

for Sara

the day the grey whale
was beached
we drove to White Rock
me retired
you laid off
you with your camera
me with a bad hip

you questioned everything
what to do with your life
I felt content
done with early mornings,
long commutes

a crowd gathered
an RCMP officer in full uniform
knee-deep in the ocean
protected the whale
(don't do that! I joked)

then you hiked up your jeans
waded out as far as possible
aimed your lens
your eye for detail and story
while I watched

click click click click
and knew

you are a journalist
always
hunt down (or wade out)
the story
so many stories
in you yet
only temporarily beached

Living Love

I know many fathers

I am the grandson of Archibald & Wallace
     the son of Russell
the father of Anna & Aaron
     the grandfather of
Madeleine & Mirabelle & Gwenoviere & Alexandria

I always wanted to be
    a good father
      and while
I sometimes succeeded
      I often failed too

when my children were born
     I was a young father,
an unsettled man full of desire
     to transform the world,
       to become first
     in something (anything),
to fill the hole at the center
     of an aching heart

I wanted to be a good father
     (I had some hopeful moments)
but mostly I was
     a colourful windsock

blowing with the wind's
                    capricious rhythms,
always filled with
                    an uncertain conviction
I needed to be someplace else,
                    needed even to be
                          somebody else

in my new role as a grandfather,
                    in my new relationship with
Madeleine & Mirabelle & Gwenoviere & Alexandria
I seek to be passionately present
                    with awakened awareness

with my granddaughters
                    I pour out my love
because I know nothing else

I am compelled, spell-bound even,
to love   to loving   to living love

                  as a grandfather
instead of looking for love
                    I now know
                      I need
                  to be love

                  I now live love

with flagrant and fragrant
                wildness

and always, daily,
                hope one day
                        to be
                a great grandfather

Home for the Summer

shoes are back
the wooden porch
more leather than wood
cracker crumbs
on the couches   tiny beige
counterpoint to green fabric
dishes line the counters
signal the dishwasher
still unloaded
a waiting game
coffee fallout
appears daily underneath
the cappuccino machine
a Hansel and Gretel trail
grains to the garbage
beside the unused vacuum

I tidy shop
cook and repeat
countless times
adventurous daughters all temporarily returned
frustration at the fights
but more relief
staving off loneliness

calm and quiet is precious
restful in appropriate quantities
you do need to hear yourself
talking to your soul

but requests for mending
DVDing
washing
rides
assistance with forms
plans
packing
appointments
daughter noise
daughter mess
is daughter joy

Many Ways to Write a Poem

I was going to spend
Monday writing a poem
but Mirabelle is ill
and her Papa alone
has a flexible schedule
so poetry will wait
while I wait on
my granddaughter
who needs her Papa
like a sturdy sonnet

and one day when
she reads this poem
I trust she will know
any poem I might write
could never satisfy
like this poem written
quickly in the gaps
of a few moments
while she slept fitfully
curled in my arms

p
o
scrabble
t
r
y

I am writing this in bed
like Edith Wharton
not yet flinging pages
to the floor
for later arrangement
Edith's process
perhaps I will invent
something new
cutting up the words
throwing them into the air
how do they land
on carpet canvas?
a Picasso poem
closing my eyes
letting the written word
careen across a page
a sheet even
or poetry scrabble
each letter of each word
assigned a score
the winning poem published
on the Scrabble ™ app
where players move letters
form new words   poems

a never-ending board of trade
till bored of trade
we all get out of bed
face the day
the blank page
the next poem
ps. I have copyrighted these ideas©

Driving Lessons

We have driven miles together, you and I,
but soon you will have your own license,
and you will not need me beside you:

> *check your blind spots*
> *don't speed*
> *watch out for other drivers*
> *look down the road*
> *watch the crosswalks*
> *look both ways*
> *turn off the signal light*

This evening in early September
you cut a curb too close,
braked hard before an amber light
you hadn't seen, made an unsafe turn.

I barked. I didn't mean to.
Finally I looked at you, not the road.
You were driving blind, the wipers
useless in a torrent of tears.

I said, I'm an ogre of a father.
You said, No, you're a good daddy.

> *Once for Necktie Day at school,*
> *you borrowed all my neckties,*
> *and your mother explained,*

She is taking neckties for her friends
who don't have fathers.
I was glad I had neckties,
even if I don't wear them anymore.

We parked on the side of St. Alban's Road
and ate Nuffy's donuts,
then under a full moon
wound our way through Richmond.

I am teaching you
how to drive,
but you are teaching me
how to be a father.

Teacher

for Rebecca

like old times
I sit in the school lobby
waiting
instruments once again
cleaned   encased
this young woman
whose notes are in my blood
on the wind

earlier she chatted animated
with students
her mentor
well on her pedagogical transformation
to teacher
marshalling teenagers with instruments
into rows or on stage
an admonishing tap
on a shoulder
a laugh at a comment
synchronized with her mentor
she assists
organizes
plays with the band
that gorgeous low thrum
of her contrabassoon

resonating through
her students' melodies

this but a prelude
of what's to come
I imagine her
in a band room many years ago
working a shammy
through the neck
of a brown and silver instrument
soaking up the spittle
or last year, those sensitive hands
on stage at her recital...

and she emerges
dry
glorious
about to burst into song
teacher-to-be

Plumb Line

yesterday I prayed
father to father,
stripped bare talk,
not in your will,
only what I wanted,
an unadorned plea,
in stark contrast to
my typical entreaties
of sham equivocation

yesterday I prayed
for my daughter
and her unborn baby,
prayed without poetry,
just a couple fathers
who have known
their share of grief,
hearing one another
as if for the first time

yesterday I prayed
with a paring knife
pressed into the heart,
tourniquet knotted,
a grenade pinched,
ready, the pin curled
around a finger, still,
God's faithfulness
true as a plumb line

Dazzling Stripes

today I meet with two women
from Beijing
here to learn
about our Kindergartens

what would they say
about yesterday?
I sat with Hayden
who draws zebras
write for me, he demanded
instead we wrote together
his "i" first,
then an admission:
he's worried about the letters
facing the wrong way

oh, everyone does that at first
I tell him
I did too
don't worry about it now
get your ideas down

I write less
Hayden writes more
he spells zebra perfectly
I tell him where to find
more books on zebras

today I meet with the two women
from Beijing
I will tell them about zebras
dazzling stripes
like unformed letters
calling to small boys

Prodigal Father

for Aaron

After I left my family with plaintive platitudes about following
my heart and pompous promises of happy endings, my son never
spoke a cross word to me, and on sacred Sunday afternoons,
he took the bus from Steveston to Kitsilano to visit: a film on
Granville, lunch in the Cactus Club, pool in the Commodore, a
caramel macchiato at Starbuck's, because like a poem that can
be composed in endless shapes, his heart is capacious. I had my
stories to live and he let me live them, glad for the time we had
together.

He phoned every night, wherever he was, wherever I was, to
tell me about *The Simpsons* or Katherine Monk's movie review,
always writing a definition of love: he let me go, and he wouldn't
let me go, through spring summer autumn winter, a cycle of
seasons like a blizzard blur, though I still saw my son seeing me.
It rained often, was often cold, my son never seemed adequately
dressed as if he did not care for clothes, did not care if he was
cold. His heart breathes wide; I breathe easily around my son.
He knows hard light; he knows the light heart.

My son and I love movies. We find our way lost in movies, the
celluloid chimera born in the spinning reels of reality out of
light, lines, and language. In his latest movie script two
characters with super powers, a hero and a villain, long past
their stories, alone in a seniors' home, remember the old days,
how they lived balance together. To be in balance is to be
suspended, hanging in the air on a fulcrum, complementary,

walking a tightrope swinging in the air, connected to the same
focus, mobile, in motion—as one moves, the other moves, like a
film is balanced with a beginning and an ending, all the parts
in relation so the whole bears the light like a net of infinite
diamonds reflecting one another infinitely.

And every Sunday when he took the bus from Howe and Smythe
to return home, no longer my home, I knew the same ache. From
week to week, the hole in the heart only grew, till one Sunday
afternoon I knew I couldn't say good-bye again. The sky was
clear, tulips burst in concrete boxes on every corner, cherry
blossoms rained. I knew only time would heal nothing; the ache
of separation from my son would only grow. My son loves me;
I love my son—a light line of balance suspended on the
semi-colon like a semi-sweet chocolate heart.

Old Dogs

semi-sarcastic tones
hang in the air
between the open fridge
(give me a goddam minute
to close the frickin' door)
& the necessity of asking
for her work schedule
to be repeated
(stop talking to me
like an Alzheimer's patient
I have a PhD
you mumble sometimes
talkfast
I have other things on my mind)

like the marking I need to do
cleaning up the dog barf
in my room
it's not like she's helping
with much these days
the dog's getting old
like me
I'm not barfing on carpet
yet
that's sure to come

I'm not looking forward
to the standard of care
if this interaction
is anything to go by

U-Haul Truck

I'm stretched out on my daughter's
Serta Perfect Sleeper,
propped up with a million feather pillows,
late afternoon, the day after Thanksgiving.

Both lazy and queasy, we drink
McDonald's strawberry milkshakes
while watching *Days of Our Lives.*
The big question: can we trust
The National Enquirer?
Will John really die?

I recall how, years ago,
on a sunny Saturday in September
I drove a U-Haul truck
down long congested Granville Street
from our home in Steveston
to Anna's new home in Kitsilano.

Since I was old enough
to rent a truck
I was the designated driver,
a reluctant Loomis courier,
conscripted to deliver
my daughter and her bed
to an apartment where
her boyfriend waited with a grin.

Nick and I heaved
the Brobdingnag bed
into his Lilliputian apartment
where it ate everything
like a voracious Godzilla.

Now I'm lounging on the bed,
the same bed that a few weeks ago
in August I helped carry back
from Kitsilano to Steveston,
to Anna and Nick's new home
(stories need no other compulsion
than the physics of inertia
and hardy hope).

The joyful news of pregnancy
turned on the lathe hit a knot
like mountain mahogany
and the whole apparatus
of fear and prayer
(understood any way
your theology leans),
kicked in with ER urgency,
each completed day of bed rest
spelling one more sturdy yarn
knit into a scarf for winter warmth.

As a father I know only
I never get much right,
just muddle through
the day like Mrs. Dalloway,
the days of our lives always

filled with enough twists
and turns to guarantee
there will be few nights
of certain perfect sleep
even on a Serta.

After more than two decades
of yearning for Marlena
while sparring with the DiMera's,
John will end his contract,
but his fiction is his,
not ours, and lying
on my daughter's bed
drinking another milkshake
while we wait, I know I will
wait as long as I need to,
with a grin or grimace,
while the sand falls
through the hour-glass,
for the U-Haul truck
full of stories I can't control.

My Canine Poet

all pumped
my book launch
the power of words
the poet laureate, a mentor
in attendance

for minutes I felt like Atwood
people lined up
the laureate shows me
how you cross out your typed name
write it in
a tradition I am proud to claim
like saying the Scottish play

for minutes I felt like
a Capital P Poet
and then—

shit everywhere when I get home
our blind old poodle couldn't wait
and so he writes me
scatological reminders of humility
on the rug
malodorous tracks in carpet

I can read what he is messaging me
down the long hall
up the stairs
under the bed

it's about patterns of documentation
recording lives so nothing is lost
not fleeting fame or attention
but the parts that may smell
are difficult to clean up

it's about bodily needs
staving off loneliness
what you can't see
that requires affirmation
and in the end
a lot of poop artistically dropped
is a kind of poem too

Smiley

at fifty-nine
I have finally
        caught up
with the smiling face
of the '70s iconic,
        perhaps ironic,
certainly ubiquitous
wide-eyed Greek
comic mask, once
long ago, pinned
to my bedroom wall

the mask first born
in 1953, my year too

I am happy
        I am having a nice day

when young,
Lana asked me
        often
if I would ever
be happy

        after years
of grumpy responses
she stopped asking

now I am old
with enough aches
& brokenness
to remind me
          constantly
my biological
& chronological
          sixty is just
around the corner

& knowing so
many who had
          no chance
to turn the corner

I am happy
          I am having a nice day

like a tightrope walk
on the braided threads
of the heart's light
I walk the curriculum
          of delight
with a precarious poise
between emotions
          & emoticons
Forrest Gump's muddy face
& Wal-Mart's sales job

conscious
        conscientious
even conscientized

by pop culture's
facile philosophy
without a conscience
to sell me anything
I will sell myself
        for

I am happy
        I am having a nice day

how has
        happy happened?

AND INFIRMITIES WILL OF COURSE INCREASE

And then I am 47:
yes;
and infirmities will of course increase.
—Virginia Woolf, *Room of One's Own*

Questions for Virginia

Virginia—
if you had not walked
into water
laden with stones
would your hips
have given out
like mine
would you have
looked into mirrors
loose skin
disappearing eyebrows
loping gait
yellow teeth some kind
of zombie apocalypse refugee

were you thinking:
best to skip this stage
the weight of those stones
unbearable
leaving Leonard
to face that reflection
all of us wondering
if only...
you shouldn't have...

there was more, Virginia
much more

not all of it
weight bearing
some lightness
of being
still purpose
laughter

Textual Affair

for Virginia Woolf

I met you when I was almost twenty, already
dead more than thirty years. Four decades
passed, I am fifty-nine, your final age.

I first met you with Mrs. Dalloway
who spent her day planning a dinner party,
all life re-presented in small events.

For the first time I knew we lived
in the ordinary, wrote the common
explosive with moments of meaning.

Through a long winter I read you
over and over, my wife complaining,
You spend more time in bed with her than me.

I met your friends too: Edith Sitwell
Vita Sackville-West Elizabeth Bowen
Rosamond Lehmann Ivy Compton-Burnett.

Now I write essays about gender and patriarchy,
poems about women I have known or not,
fiction about my father filled with questions.

For four decades you have dwelled with me
while I write poems and essays in my own room,

and your words continue to unsettle my answers.

A long time ago I was enchanted with you,
the beginning of a long quest to know,
but still I confess I know little, almost nothing.

These Women

I am making a list
women in middle age
who rose
no, floated
to that cliché ceiling
and seeing their image there
double chin
lines around the neck
skin tags
the first signs
of flabby arms & wiry
stray black hair
in their chin
like some crone

were grateful
for the occasional
blur of progressive lenses
determined, strong
mindful of lost time
took their place there
with fierceness
only years of invisibility grow

Swallow Light

In September trapped sun, for the first time,
Carrie and I sat on her back porch, and talked
about growing old and holding fast to life.

My mother said, *Learn to be happy.*
I almost asked,
What is the curriculum of joy?
but I didn't want to sound like Mr. Rogers.

Recalling childhood is like swallows
flying light in a blackberry bramble.

For our mother's birthday, my brother and I once bought
a beer mug from Woolworth's, a wild woman's image,
wide grin, flared nostrils, like the monstrous other that scares
Abbott and Costello in *Africa Screams*, and my brother and I
carried our amazing find to Carrie who aped our glow, even
though we then knew she'd never win an Oscar.
She still has the mug.

Remember Maxine Porter?
In middle age, she said, I have wasted much of my life.
I don't want to waste any more. I hope I have the heart for life.

She told me about Canada Day, how she went
to Margaret Bowater Park and amidst the crowds
celebrating, saw no one she knew.
One time, I knew everybody in Corner Brook.

She knows the peril of a long healthy life,
the memory seared in longing.

Carrie said, *Stuart Stuckless joined the circus, hurt his back,
got a settlement, everything taken into account, he did well.*

On Wednesdays when Carrie baked bread she wore
faded blue mauve pink panties on her head to prevent
stray hairs falling into the dough, and the kitchen window
always steamed up, the world condensed, hidden.

*You can never have enough life
to do all the things you want to do.*

Carrie told me stories about other mothers
like she was seeking the ingredients for a stone soup
we might enjoy together in late lean winter days.

*When Daisy Parsons got Alzheimer's,
her sons Fred and Ted cared for her
like two nurses on Dr. Kildare.
They couldn't put her in a home,
they needed her old age pension.*

Memory is a winter window, stained frost, light etched lines.

*Every Sunday Francis Dove's mother went to church.
Francis parked his car at the bottom of Lynch's Lane,*

slid his mother down the hill on a piece of linoleum,
the neighbours always said, Like a saint, nothing stops her.

I grew up on winter weekends eating moose meat stewed
long and tender, and my mother's homemade bread
spread with Good Luck margarine and Demerara molasses,
mouthfuls of sticky soft sweet steam.

Did you know if you eat a lot of beets you will pee red
and scare yourself half to death with fears of death?

Like the pond skater knows shadows, fissures, vibrations,
the resonant text read hypertextually, poised between
sun and night, I no longer know the way back, but
Carrie's wisdom like fridge magnets might guide me still:

always remember to forget
          what you don't know won't hurt you
always remember somebody nice
          kindness somehow stays with you
be open to new ideas
           we're getting older like everybody else
be nice to want nothing
          everything is good

As a boy Carrie always bought me McGregor Happy Foot socks.
The other day I bought a pair. I might even take up dancing.

Erasure

my mother asks me for my recipe
"those delicious tarts"
a compliment a daughter should cherish, right?
something inside me shatters
the recipe is hers
this another bit of erasure
along with the clothesline
she used for 50 years

in what winds do these hanging memory lapses blow,
I wonder
as they freefloat
as the frontal lobe breaks apart
the most delicate of pastries
walnuts and raisins spilling
all over the universe
too scattered to ever
measure whole again

Bread

Carrie sent me to Carter's Store for a loaf
of white sliced bread, and on my way home
through Sam Mercer's yard, Frankie Mercer,
my cousin, crazy from birth, chased me,
  at least threatened to chase me, and I ran
    like Roger Bannister with a baton under my arm, really a loaf of bread,
    and at least half the slices squeezed out, and I gave my mother what was left,
    not much, and even that mangled into obtuse angles, and she glared at me
    with the look that fills some mothers when they want to strangle you
  but can't remember your name, and hiding behind
the living room window drapes I saw Frankie
in his backyard, eating bread with tart red currant
jelly, slice after slice after slice, and now, old,
I am wheat intolerant, in a body that won't forget

My Mother's Linens

I fold tablecloths & napkins
a family dinner
it's a soothing motion
matching linen corners
women's hands over hands
always smoothing things over

there is satisfaction
in these movements
a contentment
in the rhythms
the connections between
one dinner & another
one generation & another

I love these linens
the way they fill my drawers
my mother
my heart
in the ones I choose
to lay out

busy hands
caressing lives
still folding
folding

the cloths in my mother's hands
no longer hers
the motions cradle her
like I cannot
over & over
smoothing

Tough as Nails

on her way to meet
Sue for their morning walk
Carrie stepped out her door
    fell
in the January snow

nobody   anywhere

she doesn't recall
if she fell   slow
    or hard
found her way
back into the house
phoned 911   and

her neighbours
Bern and Eva
to let them know
when the ambulance
    roared
into the cul-de-sac
there was nothing
    to worry about

in emergency
multiple tests
found nothing
    wrong

home again
   the phone
rings like a call centre
   with children
here   and there

tough as nails
   says Aaron

when I phone
she reminds me
   today is
Dad's birthday
(fourth since he died)

she is sure he is
looking out for her
   calling us all
together on his birthday

then tells me
   about Muriel
who described
her colostomy so colourfully
in medical textbook detail

Carrie is sure
she can now perform one

my mother in scrubs

wielding the scalpel
    like a baton of
delirious precision

I wish I was there
    with her
teasing the crossword
calling out to Alex Trebek
Pat Sajak   Vanna White
performing a colostomy

Exercising with My Mother

in our chairs
we raise our arms
turn our ankles
fold one hand
over the other
brain-based exercise
for the old,
wheelchair ridden,
the feeble,
me

seated beside my mother
and the world's largest
big screen TV
you couldn't miss this one
even with cataracts

knees up
1 2 3 4
5 6 7 8
8 7 6 5
4 3 2 1

it's surprisingly vigorous
our leader Vivian tells us
the chair is our friend
between tapping
a couple of men awake

asks my mother
to lead us in song

you are my sunshine
my only sunshine
she still knows the words
sings so sweetly
you make me happy
when skies are grey
her voice one function
that hasn't abandoned her

Vivian tells me
my mother comes to class
every day
what? my mother asks
where?
barely lifts her feet
off the ground
the chair her friend

Tsunami

for many years,
    decades even,
 I was restless,
    wrestling with desire
        bigger
than a sumo wrestler,
    lost in a labyrinth
      with twisted pathways
tantalizing adventures,
        potential plot lines
I pursued
    with tenacity
        but
      little perspicacity

I always imagined
    something more
      momentous than
the present moment
    I was aching toward,
and in all my longing
      for the stories that might
just lie around the corner,
    I failed to see how
      the past was stacking up
like a tsunami of
  missed moments
      twisted turns
        delirious decisions

This Is What It all Comes To

gumming cookies
I soften for her in tea
her teeth in a container
on the table
mouth and mind unwilling
the teeth an irony of centrepiece

she is hungry
I cut crusts off an egg sandwich
hand her tiny pieces
wonder if it hurts
to chew with gums
she is back to baby

the woman who shakes and shakes
approaches her babble
either foreign or nonsense
I can't tell
pat-pat-pats me on the back
folds in the tag on my shirt
I feel her longing
solicitude a tribute of sorts
she knows the tenuous
mother-daughter bonds

in a surprising burst of lost language

my mother asks
for a solution
high-vocab-speak for drink
later I rub her shoulders
the only conversation
she truly understands
she tells me
stop picking
I am back to baby

Resurrection Plant

for Vivian

on the summer day
my life was spinning
out of its orbit
and I could claim
no line of gravity,
my mother-in-law

reached out and touched
a flower in her garden,
this is the resurrection plant
because regardless
how much you cut it back
it always grows again

A THOUSAND PITIES

It would be a thousand pities if women wrote like men,
or lived like men, or looked like men,
for if any two sexes are quite inadequate,
considering the vastness and variety of the world,
how should we manage with only one?
—Virginia Woolf, *Room of One's Own*

Never Cry Woolf

A man is terribly hampered
and partial in his knowledge
of women, as a woman
in her knowledge of men.
                    —Virginia Woolf

    my friend Mo told me
she fears the men
      she meets alone at night.

she asked me what men fear.
  I wanted to say getting up
      in the morning

but I told Mo a story instead
    about how I hurt
a woman I loved.

Mo's eyes understood
my fear, my onyx nightmare,
    my fear of failure.

I told Mo how I always wanted
    to be a wild man
  dancing a tightrope tango

with words for weaving
    a safety net in the air
        or a stairway to earth.

for a long time, Mo said
    nothing, nothing at all,
then, *hold fast to the words.*

Yes, Renee, There Is a Virginia Woolf

when my high school teacher
caressed my arm
eyes gleaming power and authority
in chalkdust classrooms
when a man
held me too close
behind shoebox rows in warehouse offices
when I walked down dark streets alone
elbow jostled
till I ran to restaurant phones
calling taxi saviours
no one told me
said you were waiting
I used to read a book a night
somehow missed the W's
was I really listening
born under a rosebush
dreaming my way through
years of life
or did someone forget
to tell me
mention by the way
did you hear about Virginia
know she was waiting
would stir me to write
the ache welling
spilling on the poetry
the psychic children

who hid that row
 of W books from me?

I ate 6 Austen novels
and a 7th completed
for a woman's magazine
inhaled the Brontes
waited for Godot
searched for the author
with those 6 characters
visited that absurd zoo
howled with Allen
was afraid of George's
big bad Woolf
spent time in the children's hour
but I never found
the W's
for years
a lifetime to catch up on
catch my breath from
catch on to

yes, Renee, there is a Virginia Woolf
she lives in all your severed parts
doing dishes between lectures
putting phantom children to bed
a trace of tears
on all Shakespeare's sisters' cheeks
walking down autumn Oxbridge paths
to airless rooms
filled with folding walls
wide windows curtainless

against the summer glare
or hammerpelt of rain
writing lives a penny a piece
buried under children's stories
three little pigs
and big bad Albeean wolves

I walked past an office door one day
saw Virginia hanging on the wall
and knew
she was in my life

Lessons About Love (Not) Learned in School

In the beginning
of the decade
before the one
before this one,
a long time ago,
like yesterday,
you and I skated
all summer, a bonfire
of blue days.

I wore vertical stripes of lime
and horizontal stripes of lemon,
a clown with no balance,
while you wore the sun
tight with a low neck
and a scooter skirt with no horizon,
the most beautiful woman
I had ever seen even though I had seen
you every day of high school.

You had just lost Jimmy.
No one loves dogs like you.
You called Jimmy
and you called
and you called,
but Jimmy didn't come.
I came instead,
Jimmy's substitute,
a poor substitute perhaps.

In high school geography
we learned about faraway
places, bright colours
on a map, even the many
places we have lived,
but no textbook records
the places you and I have
seen together, places
beyond the lines of a map.

In high school history
we learned dates and facts,
but we did not learn the line
that unites the past and present.
Now we remember also to forget.
Our present to one another
is to live in the present.
Together we have learned
to taste the moment's savoury.

In high school grammar
we learned the parts of a sentence,
separate, isolate,
but together we learned
how to write the parts
so the sentence
is whole. Together
we can be all parts of the sentence,
both subject and predicate.

In high school literature
we learned the poems of dead poets.
We did not learn to write
poems. We knew no poets.
You ask me why I do not
write you more poems,
but you and I live a poem,
a long lyrical poem
without end.

In high school geometry
we learned to divide the world
into points lines planes.
We did not learn
to take the measure of the world,
to listen for the rhythm of the world.
You and I are two angles,
acute, complementary,
composing a right angle.

Through many years
we have stood side by side,
writing a right angle,
a poem without end,
the sentence whole,
our story grounded in now,
knowing the place
where our feet stand firm
with the promise of beginning.

A Poem, for the Record

for Don

don't write a poem about me
your warning words
like the writer I met
at a conference
whose partner said:
I will sue you

but I am writing you a poem
anyway
one that records
your gasp
you cried: oh, God, no
a daughter hit a wood dresser
such frightening force

a poem that remembers
you sobbed
in your basement workshop
when your brother died

a poem that recalls
how you uncomplaining
changed the dressing
on my weeping incision

a poem that writes
no, sings you

nothing to sue here

Pumpkins

on an autumn day
keen as a prism
we cut the pumpkins
in our garden,
turned the soil
which had grown
memories through
spring and summer

when the pumpkins were cut,
sorted by the children,
mine   yours   jack-o'-lanterns   pies,
you watched me hoe the barren garden
and asked, Will you ever leave me?

at the time an odd question
since I never spoke of leaving,
had nowhere to go, no wish to go,
but cutting pumpkins
on an autumn day
you saw the future
I could not, would not

Recovering Rapunzel

a new hip
slows time
less to do when you can't bend
more to do with the basics
like walking

my daughters cream my chapped legs
I'm not allowed to reach
the OT tool is only good
for picking up lint & spiders

my husband prepares meals
retrieves my fallen cane
again & again
grateful I still dream
of toast the way I like it

trapped in my prison bedroom
like Rapunzel
without the long hair & tower
(that tool
would not have helped her either)

finally I descend 13 stairs
check the disarray
on the main floor
go on short chaperoned neighbourhood

cane walks
shopping with daughters

think of poor Rapunzel
those stone walls
all that hair
no husband
no daughters

Roller Coaster

I said, You are so beautiful,
Joe Cocker like,
without the raspy strain,
more breathy wonder,
and you responded,
Your eyes aren't very good.

met at 13
dated at 16
engaged at 19
married at 20

broke your heart at 43

married again at 44
now love you
as I always intended
glad at 59

All I know is when you bend
to buckle your sandal, long
lean legs stretched out,
your dress pushed up,
I can't recall ever seeing
another more beautiful.

Dance

I strain my arms upward
hair blossoming wild in the wind
of your welcome embrace
                    full of bewilderment

I lift my face
eyes closing tight in the dark
our bodies entwisted
                    yearning

I part my lips
head moving side to side in the storm
of your cheek rough on mine
                    full of gentle force

   I am lost in the mist
   searching my forgotten self
   calling her to forge a path through
                    the abyss
   urging her to scale the brambles to
                    the peak

   calming her when she cries
   she has danced this dance before
   whispering to her when she hears
   an insistent knock on the door
   lamenting with her when she sings
   bereft because she hides no more

arms hair face eyes lips head body
      rising above
      the haze of love

      disappearing

            full of grace

I want to run with the wolves
I want to be a wolf again

Riviera Maya

the Caribbean is
          never
            still

four Australian girls
in sun-wrinkled bikinis
   sprinkle bread
     in the waves
for hungry angelfish
  (they've never learned
  they shouldn't eat wheat)

while four jealous gulls
     call out
their sense of offense
     the girls aren't
throwing
     bread in the sky

the girls raise their arms
  to cover
  their heads
in case the gulls
  bomb them
with angry shit

in a swimsuit like James Bond
    I lie on the coral beach
  almost naked

with many other people
  almost naked

we don't speak
  we don't even nod
yet we are all watching
  at least most
    of the time
all glad to be here

I keep peeking at Lana
  in her bold bikinis
still amazed we first met
as children   now parents
and grandparents   filled
  with a long   longing
desire   always   surprises

had a recurring dream
    last night   scheduled
      for a poetry reading
but couldn't find
    my poems
  like I don't know
where they are   perhaps
  lost them somewhere
between Vancouver
  and Cancun

old men are fragile
  flabby   fit

for little, hardly as fit
    as a fiddle

we old men all look
the same   except
one old man struts by
        in a thong
    brave imagination
even if I recommend
    letting imagination
        do its work

a pelican hovers
    dives into the sea
hopeful for breakfast
    much like a poet

seized by the sea
    I might yet see the sea
the aqua sea
    like the Sheaffer fountain pen
I used in grade 7
        to write essays
    never poetry

All Texted Out

patient
we teach him
text message communication
a California holiday
a way to connect
while we shop
he waits

howdoyoumakespacesagain?

where r u?

how much longer?

how much longer?

letsgonow

how much longer will u b?

letsgo

u said 5 min 30 min ago

letsgo

i won't hold this lemonade 4 u anymore

i threw the lemonade out

i'm ready 2 go

letsgo

letgo
go

Larimar

the other morning
I stepped out of the shower
in a typical rush to leave,
and you swept in,
just risen from bed
in a nightie like larimar,
with hair tousled,
offering a kiss,
and I heard the ceiling fan
like echoes of the sea faraway
on Dominican beaches

another morning soon after
you stepped out of the shower
wearing only a scar
(a cyst doctors insisted
was cancer, driven out
by steadfast imagination)
and a small silver cross
on a chain like a lariat
you wound around my neck
like a gentle noose, more
beautiful even than that day

we first knew each
other when only thirteen
(surely if any are lucky,
this is a lucky number)

how the familiar so
readily, steadily surprises
(four decades can be held
only gratefully in a poem)

legend contends larimar
heals, helps us see
like the light Caribbean Sea
washes us from the inside out

Mojave

between the buttes
red rock outcroppings
relentless wavy heat rises
amidst stunted cactus

pieces of glass inexplicably
placed by the highway
glint in the tortuous sun
like us

the Virgin River stone dry
you could walk its winding route
die of thirst
mountains look
more like dried out hills
dead weed
not the tree green
we know

between the buttes
all this heat and haze
searing sun
this dry hell fury
where all that grows
is a concrete highway
the backs of trucks
your tongue hanging
face dripping
soul exposed

Suspended Question

In any season, any place,
your one persistent question,
your only question, lingers:
why did you return?

> (I know only how
> language works as I work
> with language and language
> works with me.)

To answer the question,
I would need to confess
a narrative so tangled
in knots, any explanation
would defy deciphering.

> (Always so sure I must
> hide away from
> granite-edged truths
> that can excise the tongue.)

I will likely never speak
the truth unless in a poem
where everything I write
is always a psalm of fiction.

> (I could embed a lot of
> marginal comments here
> in order to avoid confessing

the absolute story
without absolution.)

In 2000, on the verge
of the new millennium,
we remarried with hope in the air
like a telegram without stops,
breathless with spelling the news.

    (How long can I promise
    without parenthetical
    compromise that conceals
    the story that should,
    or should not, be revealed?)

Even years later I still can't tell
you why I returned even though
you think it is so important,
and it must be, since I ask in any
season, any place, why I left.

The Day the Music...

drove in my Soul
(ironic car name)
CD in the slot
mood lights flash
purpleorangeblueyellow
Renee's faves
a gift of time
from a daughter
chronicle my past seasons
dragonfly inside a jar
of lyrics that conjure
children in the morning
first love forlorn
listening over and over
a drunken midnight choir
the day the music died
the day I first learned
the ache of relationship
say I'm a dreamer
the day the towers fell
the day I realized
it's still a man's world
clouds in my way
but the music
of the night
can re-call the rising sun
the cold night
without a sleeping bag
the way that guitar player

arrogant, worried
I might be interested
all I cared about
was the music
the season turn, turning
dragonflies
in the arms of an angel
what if God was not
one of us?
was the music
the ache
the rising sun
the night

*With gratitude and admiration for Leonard Cohen, Dan McLean,
Andrew Lloyd Webber & Charles Hart, Joni Mitchell, the Byrds, John
Lennon, Joan Osbourne, Sarah MacLachlan, and whoever wrote House
of the Rising Sun (a woman?).*

PUTTING IT INTO WORDS

I make it real by putting it into words...
It is only by putting it into words that I make it whole...
—Virginia Woolf, "Moments of Being"

The Valley

cows & chickens smell
this in contrast
to fluorescent fields
aglow on a fine Spring day

driving
down the highway
100 kilometres per hour
of self-confidence
I am about to embark
on a new venture

full of plans
I taste satisfaction
the wind rocks my car
a crazy arrhythmic mother
sounds like exhalation

the grip of my hands
on the wheel
belies my joyful approach

the smell lingers
a warning

Teacher's Pet

My boots are muddy
from hikes on the dike
with Mr. Burns

who reminds me
that everything
is worth studying:

the blackberry brambles
that horde their purple hearts
with sensible jealousy

the wet brown grass curled
around the sign posts like
malnourished garter snakes

the ducks in the slough
laughing to one another
with their funniest stories.

Mr. Burns keeps his nose
close to the ground as though
he is myopic, but really

he just wants to be near
the earth, catching the story's
scent with his big ears.

Did You Teach Today?

my mother asks
every time I visit
over and over
it is the semantic thread that runs
through our conversations
what binds us
to the leftovers of fried memory
linguistic linguine
how I imagine
the plaque in her frontal lobes

how could you come today?
didn't you have to teach?
defined by that
forever in time a pedagogue
though I am between students
between institutions
between ambitions

my mother's friends
listen closely around the tea table
they seem to retain more
of what I say
do they notice inconsistencies
how I rewrite the past
ignore the future
play with the present

no, I'm not at school

I was at a university
then left
(I am AWOL, resigned, fed up, broken)
did you teach today?
I'm on leave
did you teach today?
yes I left early
did you teach today?
no I got a day off

did you teach today?
prevaricate much?
think about
the one tenuous piece
of remembrance that still connects us?

my mother's friends
grateful for diversion smile
they accept
the way my story shifts
changes
reshapes

Artichoke Hearts

my friend traded her grandmother's dark rum fruit cake recipe
with a neighbour for his pasta sauce with artichoke hearts,
and served the pasta to another neighbour who said,
That's the best pasta I've ever eaten, and now I want to eat you,
and for five or six winters dropped by for heart-to-heart tête-à-têtes
with tea and tea biscuits till another neighbour had a biscuit and cut to
the business of what in the world was going on since the neighbourhood
was reeling out of orbit like *Another World*

while my friend knew, or pretended to know everybody in the small town
where everybody blows their car horns and waves like they haven't seen
you for years even though you just chatted about all the rain, snow, wind,
while shopping at Wal-Mart, and everybody stops to let you
into the stream of traffic even though there are no other cars anywhere,
and everybody knew, knew all about my friend, except her husband,
and nobody could tell him because everybody preferred to mind
their own business, everybody living the art of the choked heart

Why Aren't You in School?

my mother asks again
when I visit
I got out early
the simple answer best
you'll have to repeat it
repeat it endlessly

the truth is longer
more complicated
I haven't taught
in a school
for two years
it's questionable
whether she would comprehend
a position at a university
I don't comprehend it either
& I have all my faculties
just not the one
where I've been working
hostility, betrayal, envy
the stuff of the workplace

to my mother
I'm stuck in time
school time
a place I'd gladly time travel

instead
for an hour
I maintain the fiction
the wound

Yoke

how would my life
be different

    if

when Jesus said,
Take my yoke upon you,

I had heard,
Take my joke upon you?

I take words in the world
too literally.

like Yogi Ramacharaka
I need to learn
the science of breath

to breathe silence
the way words sing
in the spaces between
signs of the alphabet

how yug, yogi, yoke
are all joined
like a celestial joke
that pokes holes in the charades
of fakirs, mountebanks, and sleveens.

a wisdom-seeker takes up
the philosophy that yokes
jokes with the breadth
of life's breath, nothing less.

Snakes, My Children

in China
a man raised cobras for money
their venom in demand
until 160 of them escaped
amongst the villagers
slithering into outhouses
huts and fields

the government declared
the problem was solved
announced the errant snakes were gone
the venom released in bad decisions
blatant lies
the blindness of looking the other way
a parable for our times

my children,
once in a Chinese village
there were and there were not
cobras
that could sting the people with venom
until an official
with a cell phone in his pocket
and a warning in his eye
a man who could and could not see
assured the villagers
the snakes were not a threat

one killed
159 removed
very small anyway
thus less than deadly

my children,
this is the way snakes learn to live among us
crawling between false words
licking the poison in human tongues

Light Echoes

I jam with the wild lunacy
of the wind tangled in alders,
the day's light in the aspens

&

silence spilled in the forest's arteries
spells the heart's endless desire

&

as the sun falls lower and lower,
the sun chants and I chant with the sun
in ancient blood rhythms

&

in the whirligig of wild imaginings
I breathe raucous ramblings with no anchor point
like a deflating balloon that never runs out of air

&

the lyrical light fall of rain remembers
the morning star in a heather-blue sky

&

these rhythms are the flow of blood,
breath, breathing, breath-giving,
the measure of the heart, knowing
the living word to inspirit hope, even
in the midst of each day's busy chaos

Planting Hope

white & purple pansies
blue & white pot
Spring
newly cleaned patio stones
& dill
aromatic forerunner to pickles
lemon balm
to keep mosquitoes at bay

the furred leaves between my fingers
emit the smell of yellow
blue green
the colours of my poet heart a-healing
from a bitter year

I buy herbs & flowers
new glasses
books & books
more books to read
to vision what's ahead

we plant
and hope
and read

"we read so as not to feel alone"
(C.S. Lewis in *Shadowland*)

Between the Lines

I was riding the bus.
I was reading *Three Guineas*.
The bus stopped.
A man boarded.
His eyes were wild.
He sat beside me.
He smelled drunk,
seven in the morning.
I felt his stare.
I felt scared.
I glanced at him.
He said, *Good book.*
I read it years ago.
The book is all
between the lines,
that's where you
must read it.
He pulled the cord.
He left the bus.
He taught me
how to read Woolf.

THE RELATION BETWEEN

That perhaps is your task—
to find the relation between things that seem incompatible
yet have a mysterious affinity,
to absorb every experience that comes your way fearlessly
and saturate it completely so that your poem is a whole,
not a fragment;
to rethink human life into poetry...
—Virginia Woolf, "Letter to a Young Poet"

Who Is Virginia Woolf?

*By writing I am doing what is far more necessary
than anything else.* —Virginia Woolf

a question on *Jeopardy*
   an answer in Trivial Pursuit
a list of quotable quips
   a symbol   a cymbal
a stuffed Woolf
   a scholarly industry
a feminist deity

at twenty you first spoke
to me and forty years later
I still dwell with your words,
still know you write me,
know too I have only
begun to ask the questions
      I must ask

I've been reading your diaries,
and I feel guilty   you asked
Leonard to destroy your diaries
     he didn't   I'm glad

I don't want to be
one more scholar

reading your grocery
lists for deep meanings
but on March 24, 1941
you wrote in your diary:
Leonard is doing the rhododendrons
          your final entry

four days later, walking
beside the River Ouse
you filled your pockets
with stones   dropped
your walking stick
and wrote *the end*   as if
          you'd written all
the words you might write
while Leonard continued
doing the rhododendrons

Virginia Woolf's Alive and Well
And Living in a Co-op in False Creek

Virginia Woolf isn't dead
she's playing the pink guitar
writing for the sexes
rewriting women's lives
spinning through gynecological time
(untouched)
not an unlikely story
she's theorizing feminist fandango
in calypso classrooms

>   Edward
>   you're afraid of Virginia Woolf
>   scrawled on university bathroom walls
>   scrubbed universally in bathroom stalls

Virginia
menstrual minstrel
spiritual spectre
death by dying
defied

Posed and polished on pages of
Daring Doctrine
caring
Daunting Doctrine
flaunting

Escaped at last from her own round-rugged room
the kitchen of tiled time

Virginia's building
motorcycle memories
in the word workshop
composing computer programs
of centennial sentences
bungee jumping
from bookshelf to bookshelf
mass murdering
male Mensa mainbrains

Virginia isn't dead
temporizing temptress
                temporal-airily
                temper-rarely
                temporarily
                interred

Acknowledgements

I thank my family for all their loving and listening, and for letting me write parts of their lives, especially Don, Sara, Rebecca, Erin, Mike, and my machatunim Elaine and John, plus Matt and David.

Thank you to friends and colleagues for your interest and advocacy. And to Luciana Ricciutelli, Editor-in-Chief of Inanna Publications, I thank you for your extraordinary vision and support through the years and books.

Lastly, thank you Carl, who years ago first encouraged me upon my transformative writing journey. It has been an amazing process writing together.

Credits: Some of my poems have appeared in the following journals and anthologies.

In *Canadian Woman Studies/les cahiers de la femme*: "Dreaming Grandchildren"; "Last Summer of Childhood"; "Spill of Trees"; "Poetry Scrabble"; "These Women"; and "This Is What It All Comes To."

In *Contemplating Curriculum*: "Dazzling Stripes"; "Teacher"; "Home for the Summer"; "Did You Teach Today?" and "Why Aren't You in School?"

In *English Quarterly*: "Dance" and "Virginia Woolf's Alive and Well and Living in a Co-op in False Creek."

In *Educational Insights*: "Erasure" and "My Canine Poet."

In *Women's Education des Femmes*: "Yes, Renee, There Is a Virginia Woolf."

In *Mothers and Daughters* (edited by Janet MacLellan et al.): "Gardens" and "My Mother's Linens" (in press).

—Renee Norman

I thank my family, Lana, Anna, Aaron, Nicholas, Penny, Madeleine, Mirabelle, Gwenoviere, Alexandria, Kerry, Russell (Bud), Chesley, and Vivian, for all their inspiration and love, and I thank colleagues and friends for their steadfast encouragement, especially Kedrick James, Peter Gouzouasis, Karen Meyer, Rita Irwin, George Belliveau, Lynn Fels, Celeste Snowber, Pauline Sameshima, Sean Wiebe, Cynthia Chambers, and Erika Hasebe-Ludt.

Also, I thank Luciana Ricciutelli and Inanna Publications for creatively and indefatigably promoting the spirit of Virginia Woolf by honouring the efficacy of words.

Finally, I thank Renee for the countless opportunities to share poetry and grow in wisdom on a long journey of writing and living with heart.

Credits: Some of my poems have appeared in the following journals and anthologies:

In *Lip-Service Journal*: "Ten Reasons Why Your Grandfather Loves You."

In *Inkshed*: "Mirabelle" and "Many Ways to Write a Poem."

In *The Inspired Heart: An Anthology* (edited by Melinda Cochrane): "Gwenoviere" and "Roller Coaster."

In *Green's Magazine*: "Driving Lessons"; "Between the Lines" and "Lessons about Love (Not) Learned in School."

In *Journal of the Canadian Association of Curriculum Studies* (JCACS): "U-Haul Truck."

In *Perspective Poetry Magazine*: "Smiley."

In *Whetstone*: "Textual Affair."

In *Journal of the Association for Research on Mothering*: "Swallow Light."

In *Canadian Stories: Special Edition III*: "Bread"; "Resurrection Plant" and "Light Echoes."

In *The Amethyst Review*: "Never Cry Woolf."

In *The Literary Half-Yearly*: "Pumpkins."

In *Slow Trains Literary Journal*: "Larimar" and "Yoke."

In *LEARNing Landscapes*: "Teacher's Pet."

In *Existere*: "Artichoke Hearts."

—Carl Leggo

Renee Norman, PhD, is a prize-winning poet, writer, and retired educator. Her poetry book, *True Confessions* (Inanna), was awarded the Helen and Stan Vine Canadian Jewish Book Award for poetry. She is also the author of two other books of poetry, *Backhand Through the Mother* and *Martha in the Mirror* (Inanna). She received the Canadian Association for Curriculum Studies Distinguished Dissertation Award for *House of Mirrors: Performing Autobiograph(icall)y in Language/Education*, published by Peter Lang. Previously, she worked as a classroom teacher in public schools, an arts educator, a university professor, and school board consultant. She lives in Coquitlam, British Columbia.

Photo credit: Bruce McCaughey

Carl Leggo is a poet and professor in the Department of Language and Literacy Education at the University of British Columbia. His books include: *Growing Up Perpendicular on the Side of a Hill; View from My Mother's House; Come-By-Chance; Lifewriting as Literary Métissage* and an *Ethos for Our Times* (co-authored with Erika Hasebe-Ludt and Cynthia Chambers); *Creative Expression, Creative Education* (co-edited with Robert Kelly); *Sailing in a Concrete Boat: A Teacher's Journey; Arresting Hope: Women Taking Action in Prison Health Inside Out* (co-edited with Ruth Martin, Mo Korchinski, and Lynn Fels); and *Arts-based and Contemplative Practices in Research and Teaching: Honoring Presence* (co-edited with Susan Walsh and Barbara Bickel). He lives in Steveston, British Columbia.